Apple Watch Series 5 Guide for Seniors

Practical Guide to Master Your New iWatch Series 5 for the Elderly

Tech Reviewer

Copyright @ 2019

TABLE OF CONTENT

How to Use this Book

Welcome! Thank you for purchasing this book and trusting us to lead you right in operating your iWatch series 5. Be rest assured that this book has an updated list on all the current tips and tricks available for the latest addition in the Apple watch family. To better understand how the book is structured, I would advise you first read from page to page after which you can then navigate to particular sections as well as make reference to a topic individually. This book has been written in the simplest form to ensure that every user understands and gets the best out of this book. You can also use the well outlined table of content to find specific topics faster and more efficiently.

Introduction

The Apple Watch is the best gadget for time tracking, fitness, messages on the go and so many other features. This guide would show you how to set up your new Apple Watch.

The iWatch Series 5 is the latest and greatest addition to the Apple Watch family. The Series 5 Watch has an always-on display which is absent in other older versions and a built-in compass. You can also make international emergency calls on cellular models, even if you are roaming or have no active cellular plan.

The goal of this user guide is to provide you with a well referenced guide that you can always refer to when trying out new features on your new smart watch. You would find every single detail you need to optimize performance on your Apple watch written in the simplest and easy to understand format.

Chapter 1: Getting Started

How to Set Apple Watch from Scratch

Follow the steps below to set up your Watch from the scratch.

- Follow the pairing steps to pair your iWatch with iPhone.

- Then click on **Set Up as New Apple Watch.**

- Click either **Right or Left** to let Apple Watch know the wrist you plan to wear your iWatch on.

- Click **Agree** to accept the terms and conditions of watchOS.

- Then click on **Agree** again.

- Enter your Apple ID to set up Find My iPhone and Activation Lock.

- Click on **OK** as a confirmation that you understand the **Shared Settings for iWatch and iPhone.**

- Click on **Create a Passcode** to set up a passcode for your Apple Watch.

- Click on **Add a Long Passcode** to set up a passcode longer than 4 digits.

- Or click on **Don't Add Passcode** if you would rather not have a passcode on your iWatch.

- Go to your Apple Watch and click to set a 4-digit passcode.

- Input your passcode one more time to confirm.

- Choose whether you want to set up cellular on your iWatch.

- You can then choose to set up Apple Pay now or choose to set it up later. Depending on the card you are adding, it may request that you enter the entire card number or security code of your card.

- Go to your iPhone and click on **Continue** to confirm that you understand the Emergency SOS.

- Click on **Install All** to install all the watchOS apps available to your iPhone.

- Click on **Choose Later** if you would like to do this later.

- Allow some time for your watch to sync with your smartphone. While waiting, you can click on **Apple Watch Basics** to familiarize yourself with basic navigation tips on your iWatch.

How to Restore Apple Watch from Backup

- After you have paired your iWatch with iPhone, then click on **Restore from Backup** on your iPhone.

- Select the relevant backup.

- Agree to the terms and conditions.

- Enter your Apple ID to set up Find My iPhone and Activation Lock.

- Click on **OK** as a confirmation that you understand the **Shared Settings for iWatch and iPhone.**

- Click on **Create a Passcode** to set up a passcode for your Apple Watch.

- Click on **Add a Long Passcode** to set up a passcode longer than 4 digits.

- Or click on **Don't Add Passcode** if you would rather not have a passcode on your iWatch.

- Go to your Apple Watch and click to set a 4-digit passcode.

- Input your passcode one more time to confirm.

- Choose whether you want to set up cellular on your iWatch.

- You can then choose to set up Apple Pay now or choose to set it up later. Depending on the card you are adding, it may request that you enter the entire card number or security code of your card.

- Go to your iPhone and click on **Continue** to confirm that you understand the Emergency SOS.

- Click on **Install All** to install all the watchOS apps available to your iPhone.

- Click on **Choose Later** if you would like to do this later.

- Allow some time for your watch to sync with your smartphone. While waiting, you can click on **Apple Watch Basics** to familiarize yourself with basic navigation tips on your iWatch.

How to Pair your iWatch with iPhone

Although the iPhone and Apple Watch are two different hardware, but you cannot operate the iWatch without the iPhone. The first step to take with your new Apple Watch, is to switch it on and then pair it with the iPhone. You would need to use the Apple Watch app for iOS to pair your watch with the iPhone. The app is usually preinstalled in your iPhone except if you have deleted it previously, then you can install it from the App Store.

There are several ways to paint your iPhone with the Apple Watch so choose the one that suits you.

How to Automatically Pair Your New Watch with your iPhone

- Open the Watch app stores on your iPhone. (You also can place the Watch close to the iPhone to display a similar interface to the AirPods pairing screen, which would automatically start the watch app)
- Click on **Start Pairing**
- Move your iPhone over the iWatch until the iWatch is lined up in the yellow rectangle's center.

- You should receive the message "Your Apple Watch Is Paired" once the watch is paired successfully.

- You can then choose from two options to set up your Watch. Either you choose **"Restore Apple Watch from a Backup"** or **"Set up your Apple Watch from Scratch".**

How to Pair your iWatch Manually

You can manually pair your watch to your phone if you are not able to automatically pair it successfully.

Rather than using the QR code method to pair, you can use the name of your Apple Watch to begin the pairing process.

- Open the Watch app stores on your iPhone. (You also can place the Watch close to the iPhone to display a similar interface to the AirPods pairing screen, which would automatically start the watch app)
- Click on **Start Pairing**
- Then click on **Pair Apple Watch Manually.**

- Go to your Apple Watch and click on (**i**) to display the name of your device.

- Go to the iPhone and choose your Apple watch from the available list.

- You can then choose from two options to set up your Watch. Either you choose "**Restore Apple Watch from a Backup**" or "**Set up your Apple Watch from Scratch.**"

How to Pair an Existing iWatch with a new iPhone

There are no easy steps to manually back up your iWatch to the iCloud as you have with the iPhone, you either have to backup with the iPhone's iCloud or backup using iTunes. So, though your watch would regularly sync its data to your iPhone whenever you are connected to Wi-fi or Bluetooth, you still cannot choose to manually backup your details except if you now manually unpair your iWatch which would cause the watch to automatically sync its latest contents to Your iPhone backup. Whenever you want to switch to another iPhone, you have to first impair your iWatch from the old smartphone, deactivate the Activation lock and then make a backup of your iPhone. The steps below would show you how to.

There are 2 ways to prepare your iWatch to move to a new iPhone.

iCloud and Automatic Setup

Since the launch of the iOS 11.2, you can make use of Automatic setup to move both the Apple Watch and its iPhone backup to a new iPhone without having to unpair and repair. However, there are steps you must take to ensure that the move over is properly done. See the following

- Ensure that your iWatch is current by activating the iCloud Health Sync.
- Backup your current iPhone before you begin the transfer to the new iPhone.

Unpair/Repair

If you choose not to restore your new iPhone from the backup of the old iPhone, your best option to move the iWatch would be to force a backup. To do this, you have to unpair your iWatch from the current iPhone with the instruction on how to unpair.

How to Switch Your iWatch to a New iPhone

Depending on the way you set up your new iPhone, the steps would be slightly different for setting up your iWatch.

For Automatic Setup

- When setting up your iPhone, select the **Automatic Setup** option.

- As you proceed with the setup, you would get a prompt with the following "Do you want to use '[name of iWatch] with this iPhone? Click on **Continue** to confirm.

If you choose the Unpair/Repair

- Ensure you have unpaired your watch from the current iPhone.

- Choose to setup your iPhone from scratch or from an iTunes or **iCloud backup** (the steps are included in this guide)

- Once your iPhone has setup completely, launch the **Watch** app.
- Choose to setup your iWatch **from Existing backup** or **From Scratch.**

Note: if you do not want to lose your health data, you have to have enabled the iCloud health sync option as well as set up both the iWatch and iPhone from scratch.

How to Move your iWatch to a New iPhone When there is no Backup

If you want to start from the scratch on your new iPhone without any backup, you have two options to choose from.

1. If you do not mind losing your health data and other related contents, then choose to start from scratch on both the iPhone and the iWatch. When you choose this option, you would lose your health data and downloaded apps including your

GPS routes, all saved workouts, heart rate data and achievements.

2. If you want to retain your health data, you can move it to a clean install iWatch and iPhone with the steps below

- Go to **settings**

- Click on **iCloud.**

- Then toggle on the switch for **Health.**

- Allow some time for all your data to sync before you erase your old smartphone.

- Once the health data has synced then follow the steps highlighted below to set up your Apple watch.

3. Follow the guide on **Unpair/Repair** to unpair your watch.

4. After you have set up your iPhone, launch the **Watch App.**

5. And then follow the steps above to complete the setup.

How to Set the Modular Face on iWatch to Multicolored

The modular face on your iWatch is one of the most useful faces you can find on a watch. The steps below would guide you on setting the multicolored option of the modular face.

How to choose the Modular Clock Face on iWatch

You can do this in two ways. The easiest way is by using the Watch app.

- Go to your paired iPhone and open the Watch app.

- Go to **My Faces** selection to the Modular face.

- If you don't find it here, then go to the **Face Gallery** section.

- Navigate to the Modular section and choose a color you like to view it.

- Click on **Add** to include it to your faces.

- Click on your preferred Modular face.

- Navigate to the bottom of your screen and click on **Set as current Watch Face.**

If you do not have your iPhone close, then you can set this up on your Apple Watch with the guides below

- Go to the **Clock Face** of your Apple Watch.

- You can also just double press the **Digital Crown** to take you there.

- Firmly press down on the clock face to see the face switcher.

- Swipe right or left to get to the **Modular Face** option

- If you are yet to add the Modular face to your list of faces, scroll to the right and click on the **+New** button. Then scroll vertically to find the Modular face (either using the Digital Crown or by swiping). Select it and the Watch face would switch to **Modular Face.**

How to Choose the Multicolor Option for the Modular Face

This is easier done through the Watch app.

- Go to your iPhone and open the Watch app.

- Go to **My faces** and select **Modular face.**

- Scroll left till you get to the end in the color selection and then click on **Multicolor.**

- Your Modular face would set to multi-color.

Follow the steps below to set this on the Watch itself.

- Ensure that your Watch face is set to the **Modular Watch face** with the steps already discussed above.

- Then firmly press down on the watch face to see the **face switcher.**

- Click on **Customize.**

- In a counter clockwise move, Rotate the **Digital Crown** to access the **Multicolor option.**

- Once done, use the Digital Crown to exit to the face switcher and then to the clock face.

How to Setup Custom Complications for the Modular Face

- Go to your iPhone and open the Watch app.

- Go to **My faces** and select **Modular face.**

- Navigate to the color options and you would find 5 complications (Middle, Top Left, Bottom Middle, Bottom Left and Bottom Right).

- Click on the complication position you want.

- By default, the change would reflect on your iWatch instantly but you can also navigate to the bottom and click on **Set as current Watch Face** to confirm

To make this change from your Apple Watch, follow the steps below

- Firmly press down on the clock face on your watch to see the **face switcher.**

- Click on **Customize.**

- Swipe to your right to change to complications from the color option.

- Click on the complication you want.

- Rotate the Digital Crown to see all the available complications.

- Make your selection, then press the **Digital Crown** to go back to the face switcher, press it again to see the clock face.

How to Use Scribble to Send Emoji on iWatch

Scribble is the handwriting feature on the iWatch that you can use to communicate via text rather than a canned response or dictation. To do this, simply use your finger to write words on the scribble screen which would automatically turn into text that you can send to a receiver via chat rooms, iMessages, email and more

How to Convert a Word into Emoji Via Scribble

- Open the app you want to use to send the communication like Messages or Mails on your Apple Watch.
- Click on the **Conversation** you wish to send a response or firmly press on your screen to begin a new message.
- While in the conversation screen, click on **Scribble.**

- Write any word that relates to an Emoji like "Angry," "LOL," or "Poop."
- Rotate the **Digital Crown** to bring up word predictions.
- Choose the **Emoji** you want to use in the written sentence.
- Click on **Send** to deliver the communication.

You can always click on the Emoji button rather than using Scrabble, but this method is faster when trying to send a message and wish to include an emoji too.

How to Mute the Alert and Ringer on your iWatch

I have highlighted some things you should know below about your Apple Watch.

- Do Not Disturb and Silent Mode are not same thing on the Apple Watch. **Silent Mode** only silences sound which means haptics will still notify you as needed.
- **Silent Mode** does not affect timers or alarms
- When you place your hand in front of your watch, it can stop a

sound. **Cover to Mute** has to be enabled in the Watch app for this feature to work. Go to the Watch app in the iPhone, then go to **My Watch** then click on **Sound & Haptics** and enable the **Cover to Mute** feature.

How to Use Silent Mode on Your iWatch

Follow the steps below to silent your iWatch:

- Use the Digital Crown to access the Apple watch face.

- Make a swipe up gesture with your finger to access the **Control Center.**

- Move down and click on **Silent,** which has a bell icon.

Follow the steps below to activate this feature using your iPhone

- Go to the Watch App in the iPhone.

- Click on **Sounds and Haptics.**

- At the upper part of the screen, activate **Silent Mode.**

- Follow the steps when you wish to deactivate the silent mode.

How to Enable Theater Mode on iWatch

When Theatre Mode is enabled, you would still feel taps but your Watch screen will not light up as usual. Follow the steps below to enable this feature.

- Use the Digital Crown to access the Apple watch face.
- Make a swipe up gesture with your finger to access the **Control Center.**
- Navigate to the bottom of your screen and then click on the

Theater Mode button. The button looks like 2 theater masks.

- Click the Orange button for **Theater Mode** to confirm.
- Once enabled, you would see **Theater Mode: On** on top the screen in the control center. On the Watch face, you would also see the theater mask icon to show that Theater mode is currently enabled.

How to Disable Theater Mode.

- Wake your Apple Watch by clicking on it or pressing one of its buttons.

- Make a swipe up gesture with your finger to access the **Control Center.**

- Then Navigate to the bottom of your screen and click on the **Theater Mode button.** The button looks like 2 theater masks.

How to Minimize Light from Your Apple Watch Under Theater Setting

Although the theater mode would stop your watch from lighting up and buzzing unintentionally, it would however, not dim your screen or give you a watch face that is theater friendly in case you need to access your watch during a movie. So, you need to manually minimize the light with the steps below:

- First enter **Edit** mode by firmly pressing on your Apple Watch face.

- Move from right to left.

- Click on **New (+)**

- Turn the **Digital Crown** or swipe to navigate to the **Modular** watch face

- Click on the **Modular Face.**

- Firmly press on the Modular face to **edit.**

- Click on **Customize.**

- Rotate the **Digital Crown** to modify the watch face color to red.

- Swipe to the left to select your complications.

- Click on each complication and turn the **Digital Crown upward** until you have set the complication to **Off.**

- Click on the **Digital Crown** to leave the **Edit mode.**

- When done, your watch face would be black and black with just the time showing in red.

How to Find your iPhone with your iWatch

You can find your missing iPhone by using the **Find My iPhone** feature in your iWatch for times when you misplace your iPhone around the house and other places. For this to work, Bluetooth has to be enabled on the iPhone and the smartphone also needs to be turned on and this can only work for the iPhone that has been paired with your Apple watch.

- Click on **Digital Crown** to go to the watch face.

- Make a swipe up gesture from the bottom of the watch face.

- You would see your iPhone as **Connected** at the top of your screen.

- Go to the left bottom corner and click on **Find iPhone.**

- After some seconds, your iPhone would ring out with a small ping.

- Keep clicking on the button until you discover your iPhone.

Tip: the ping sound may not always be sufficient to find your phone, so you can just click and hold down on the **Find iPhone** button to make your iPhone ring as well as flash LED light.

How to Download and Install watchOS 6.0.1 on Your iWatch

- Ensure your iPhone is updated to iOS 13.

- Connect your smartphone to Wi-fi connection and open the **Watch app.**

- Your Apple Watch needs to be charged to minimum of 50% and should be connected to a magnetic charger.

- Click on **My Watch** on your smartphone.

- Click on **General.**

- Then click on **Software Update.**

- Select **Download and Install.**

- Input your **iPhone Passcode** once requested.

- Accept the terms and conditions by clicking on **Agree.**

- Go to your Watch and click on **Proceed** to start the download.

- Input the **Passcode** again on the Watch.

- The update to watchOS will download and move to your Watch while the Watch would reboot to accept the update. Once the reboot is done, then you ready to explore.

How to Confirm Your Connection

If you have issues successfully downloading and installing the updates, it could be because your phone is not connected. Follow the steps below to check this.

- Go to your iPhone and launch the settings app.

- Click on **Wi-Fi,** while doing this, check that Bluetooth is also enabled.

- Make a swipe up gesture on your Watch to display the **Control center. You would see a green** Connected icon to show that your iPhone is connected.

How to Force Quit and Restart

- Go to the iPhone and open the **Watch app.**

- Press the Home button twice to display the multitasking interface if your iPhone has a home button. If no home button then swipe from the bottom of your screen up for iPhones using Face ID.

- Swipe up on the opened **Watch App.**

- Then make a swipe up gesture on the Watch app card to force close it.

- Now, press and hold the **Side button** of your watch.

- Use the slider on your screen to **Power Off.**

How to Customize Your Control Center

The Control center of your watch works in similar way with the iPad or iPhone. You can use the buttons to quickly activate features like turning cellular data and Wi-fi off and on or enabling Airplane mode etc. You can also change how these buttons are placed to give you a faster access to the features you use most. Follow the steps below to customize your watch.

- Go to the control center on your iWatch by swiping up from the end of your screen.

- Click on **Edit.**

- For each button you want to rearrange, click, hold and pull the button to its new location in the control center.

Chapter 2: Customize Workouts for your iWatch

How to Display a Metric in Workouts for the iWatch

Every preset workout has its own default settings that decides what metrics would show on your watch screen, and you can even add options to some of them. It's important to note that you can only have a maximum of 5 metrics displayed on your watch while working out. So, you would have to first hide a metric if you already have five. Follow the steps below to customize the metrics.

- Go to the Apple watch app on your iPhone.

- Click on **My Watch.**

- Navigate down and select **Workout.**

- Click on **Workout View.**

- Select the workout you wish to modify.

- Click on **Edit** at the right top corner of your screen

- Click on the **Add button** beside the metric you wish to add.

- Then click on **Done.**

- You would now see the metric displayed on your watch screen each time you select that workout type.

How to Hide a Metric in the Workouts App

- Go to the Apple watch app on your iPhone.

- Click on **My Watch.**

- Navigate down and select **Workout.**

- Click on **Workout View.**

- Select the workout you wish to modify.

- Click on **Edit** at the right top corner of your screen

- Click the **Remove** option beside the metric you wish to remove.

- Click on **Remove**

- Then click on **Done.**

How to Reorder Metrics in Workouts

Follow the steps below to modify the order in which the metrics displays on your watch.

- Go to the Apple watch app on your iPhone.

- Click on **My Watch.**

- Navigate down and select **Workout.**

- Click on **Workout View.**

- Select the workout you wish to modify.

- Click on **Edit** at the right top corner of your screen

- Click and hold the button for **Reorder** beside the metric you want to move.

- Pull the metric to your preferred location.

- Click on **Done.**

How to View a Single Metric for Apple Watch

Choose just one metric if you like a simple interface to show when doing your workouts.

- Go to the Apple watch app on your iPhone.

- Click on **My Watch.**

- Navigate down and select **Workout.**

- Click on **Workout View.**

- Click on **Single Metric.**

Chapter 3: How to Set Up Siri

Using Siri on your Apple watch is linked to your iPhone. If you have ever enabled Siri on your iPhone, it means that Siri has been activated automatically on your watch. However, you can follow the steps below to enable Siri.

- Go to your iPhone and open the settings app.

- Click on **Siri & Search**.

- If using iPhone 8 and older versions, click on the **Press**

Home for Siri option. For iPhone X and newer versions, click on **Press Side Button for Siri** to enable Siri for the Apple Watch and iPhone.

How to Use Siri on Your iWatch

You have two ways you can access Siri. You can either use the "Hey Siri" command or just press and hold the Digital Crown and Begin your command. You need to have a strong connection whether using cellular connection on the iPhone or via Wi-fi to be able to access this feature.

Depending on how strong your connection is, it may take Siri some seconds to process your request; after you must have said your request, Siri may respond with "I'll tap you when I'm ready" or "Hang on...". You can drop your hand while waiting for feedback from Siri. When Siri finish processing, your watch would buzz you on the wrist.

How to use "Hey Siri" on your iWatch

- Lift your Apple watch close to your face. If you disabled the wrist raise option, simply click on your watch screen to wake it.

- Then say **Hey Siri** and continue with your query.

How to Manually Activate Siri on your iWatch

- Press and hold down the **Digital Crown** button.

- Call out your command or question to Siri.

How to change Siri's Voice on Apple Watch

You can change your virtual assistant's voice with the steps below:

- Go to your iPhone and open the settings app.

- Click on **Siri & Search**.

- Then click on **Siri Voice** and choose your preferred voice.

Note: You may need to connect to Wi-Fi if you want to download more voices.

How to turn off Siri's voice on iWatch

While you cannot modify the volume of the Siri's voice, you can totally deactivate Siri.

- Go to your iPhone and open the settings app.

- Click on **Siri.**

- Move the switch beside **"Hey, Siri"** to the left to disable it.

How to use the Siri with Watch Faces

You can design your own specialized Siri Watch face. Apart from giving you a customized Siri button directly on your watch face, it would also intelligently draw data from Photos, calendars and more as well as provide information like Wallet Passes and upcoming weather, to you.

How to set up the Siri watch face on your iWatch

- Lift your wrist or click on the display of your watch to activate it.

- Firmly press down on the **Apple Watch's display.**

- Rotate the Digital Crown or swipe to the left through all the watch faces until you reach the end.

- Then click on the + **button**.

- Navigate through the alphabetical list then click on **Siri watch face**.

How to set up a Siri watch face on your iPhone

You can have more control for the Siri watch face by using the watch app installed on your iPhone.

- Go to the watch app on your smartphone.

- Then click on **Face Gallery.**

- Navigate to **New in watchOS** or **Siri** option then click on **Siri.**

- Click the **Add** button

- Click on **My Watch.**

- Under **My Faces,** scroll to the left and then click on **Siri.**

- Select your **Top Right** and **Top Left** complications.

- Select your **Data Sources**.

- Then begin use by clicking on **Set as current Watch Face**.

How to use the Siri watch face

Follow the steps below to use this feature.

- Lift your wrist or click on the display of your watch to activate it.

- Click on the **Siri button** to use the assistant.

- Wind the **Digital Crown** to show cards for upcoming events, current weather, and more.

- Click on any of the displayed cards to go to the corresponding watch app.

How to Quickly and Reliably Trigger Siri

There are times Siri may not work effectively due to background noise and several other external factors. Here, I have compiled some tips to use if you want Siri to be more reliable.

- Press down on the Digital Crown button to get Siri to listen. This is most helpful if you are in a noisy place where it is hard for Siri to know when you are done speaking. Continue to hold down the Digital Crown button until you are done speaking.

- Use screen taps when using **"Hey Siri".** The Watch is configured to listen for **"Hey Siri"** only on-screen wake, in a bid to save battery. This feature can be frustrating especially if you enabled your device to wake when you raise your wrist and when you do not say your query on time. However, you can reset the process when you briefly place your palm over your watch screen to turn it off then re-lift your wrist or click on the watch display to wake your watch then follow with the Siri command.

How to use Handoff to switch from Siri on your Apple Watch to your iPhone

Handoff allows you to begin an action on a particular device and then complete it on another device. Due to the small screen size of your watch, there are some things you cannot do on the watch. If you request Siri to help, it would send you to your iPhone and transfer the request there. Follow the steps below to enable Handoff for your iWatch.

- From your iPhone, go to the watch app.

- Click on **My Watch.**

- Then click on **General.**

- Navigate to **Enable Handoff** and use the switch to activate this feature.

- With this enabled, you can ask Siri anything from your Apple Watch and if it is something that cannot be done on the watch, Siri would instantly offer to move you to your iPhone.

How to Enable Raise to Speak

You would have to first activate this feature on your iWatch to be able to enjoy it. Follow the steps below

- Go to settings in the iWatch.
- Click on **General.**
- Then click on **Siri.**
- Move the switch beside **Raise to Speak** to the right to enable it.

- Use the Digital Clock to go back home.

Activate Siri with the Raise to Speak Feature

To activate Siri via this feature, simply raise your iWatch close to your mouth then begin your command. If the iWatch is not positioned close to your Mouth, Siri would not be activated.

How to Customize Raise to Speak on iWatch

You can go through the settings to customize when and how you want Siri to respond on your iWatch. In

most cases, the setting by default is
set to **always On**.

- Go to settings in the iWatch.
- Click on **General.**
- Then click on **Siri.**
- Select from the 3 options.
  Control with Silent Mode, Always
  On, or *Headphones Only*
- If you select **Headphones Only,**
  Siri would only respond when
  the iWatch is paired with a
  wireless headphone.
- **Control with Silent Mode** option
  means that whenever the watch

is on silent mode, you would be unable to use Siri.

- You can also use the minus (-) and plus (+) sign to control the volume of Siri.

Chapter 4: How to Set up Fall Detection

The Fall detection on the iWatch series 5 helps to connect you with medical services when you fall, as long as you are wearing your watch.

Whenever you have a hard fall, the Apple Watch would automatically tap your wrist, make an alarm sound and show an alert. You can then choose if you want to alert emergency services from your iWatch or ignore the alerts.

When the fall detection is enabled, your watch would know when you are moving and whenever it detects a fall, it gives you 60 seconds to respond to the alarm after which it would automatically contact emergency services once it does not receive any response from you. Then, on your screen, a 15 second countdown would begin from the time it makes the automatic call. Feel free to click on Cancel whenever you want. Whenever the watch is able to make the contact to emergency services, persons you placed on emergency contact list would receive the information that you had a fall as well as your present location.

What Happens in an Emergency Call

Whenever the iWatch establishes a call with the emergency persons, your watch will inform the contact person through an audio message that it detected a fall. It would also provide your longitude and latitude coordinates. You would need to click on **Stop Recorded Message** before the message can stop playing. You now have the chance to speak with anyone that responds. After you have finished with the call, use the phone icon to end the call and click on **Yes** to agree.

How to Enable Fall Detection

This feature is not enabled by default except for users who are 65 years and above. You need to have included your age when setting up your watch for it or in the health app for the watch to pick your age.

- Click on the watch app from your iPhone.

- Then go to **My Watch.**

- Click on **Emergency SOS**.

- Navigate down and enable the option for **Fall Detection** by moving the switch to the right.

How to Make Emergency Call Following a Fall

After you fall and the iWatch sends an alert, your screen would display a slider to contact emergency services. You would also see an option for **I'm okay.**

- If you want to contact emergency services, pull the

slider to the right on your iWatch. Otherwise, click on **I'm okay.**

- Listen to the instructions from the service operator and so as advised.
  End the call using the phone icon once done.
- Confirm by clicking **Yes.**

How to Add Family and Friends to List of Emergency Contacts

The steps below would show you how to add emergency contacts.

- Go to your iPhone and launch the health app.

- Click on your profile at the right top of your screen.

- Click on **Medical ID.**

- Click on **Edit** at the right top corner.

- Move to the section for **Emergency Contacts,** then click on **add emergency contact** to present contacts stored on your phone.

- Click on the contacts you want to add to the list.

- Then click on the contact's phone number.
- On the next screen, confirm your relationship with the selected contact.
- Repeat these steps to add all your emergency contacts.

Important Settings for Fall Detection to Work

The wrist detection feature has to be enabled for the iWatch to be able to call emergency services automatically.

- Go to settings on your iWatch.

- Click on **Passcode.**

- Enable **Wrist Detection** by moving the switch to the right.

How to Disable Fall Detection

Apart from users 65 years and above who have indicated their age, the fall detection is not enabled by default. However, if the feature is enabled and you do not want to use it again, follow the steps below to disable it

- Click on the watch app from your iPhone.

- Then go to **My Watch.**

- Click on **Emergency SOS.**

- Navigate down and disable the option for **Fall Detection** by moving the switch to the left.

Chapter 5: How to Set up and Use Apple Pay on your iWatch

It's easier to buy something on your iWatch when you make use of Apple Pay. Here, you would learn how to add your bank cards for shopping needs.

How to Add Cards to Apple Pay

Its most important that your bank supports Apple pay service. Go to the Apple support website for details of banks that you can use on the Apple Pay. The steps below would show you how to link your bank card.

- Click on the watch app from your iPhone.

- Then go to **My Watch.**

- Click on **Wallet & Apple Pay**.

- Go to payment cards and click on **Add Card.**

- Click on **Continue.**

- Either you place your smartphone over your credit card to scan the card details or you click on **Enter Card Details Manually.**

- Input the security code for your card and click on **Next.**

- Click on **Add.**

- Then click on **Confirm** to accept your bank's terms and conditions.

- Select either Email, text message or call to receive verification message.

- Click on **Next.**

- Input the verification code received and click on **Next** again.

- Once done, click on **Done.**

- Repeat the steps for each card you wish to add.

Note: cards added to Apple Pay on your iWatch does not automatically reflect for use on the iPhone. You would need to add to your iPhone too.

How to Pay with Apple Pay

Follow the steps below to use the Apple Pay for checkouts on the iWatch.

- Double click the side button on your iWatch to make use of the default card, then hold your

Apple Watch display within some centimeters away from the contactless reader.

- Hold until you get a gentle tap to complete the payment.
- The Digital Crown would take you back to the watch face.

If you would rather use a different card for the purchase, follow the steps below:

- Click twice on the iWatch side button.
- Swipe to the right or left to select your preferred card.

- As soon as the card appears on the watch face, position your watch close to the reader to pay.
- Hold until you get a gentle tap to complete the payment.
- The Digital Crown would take you back to the watch face.

Chapter 6: Other Customizing Tips and Tricks

How to Remove and Add Complication options from the Customize screen

In your option list, you would find 3rd party apps that support complications by default. If the list seems too long, try removing some of the options with the steps below:

- Click on the watch app from your iPhone.

- Then go to **My Watch** and click on **Complications.**

- at the right upper side of your screen, click on **Edit.**

- Click the (-) **minus** button at the left side, beside the app you wish to delete from the list.

- Click on **Remove.**

- Then click **Done** once you are satisfied.

- To add a complication, go through the steps above but

click on the **(+) plus** sign instead
of the minus beside the app.

How to Customize Watch Face

Complications Using your Apple

Watch

Follow the steps below to customize
complications for every of the watch
face using the Apple watch while on
the go.

- Use the Digital crown to control
  the watch face of your apple
  watch.

- Firmly press down on the **Watch face** to go into customization mode.

- Choose a watch face.

- Then click on **Customize.**

- Make a swipe gesture to the left till you get to the last option for customization. That is the complications menu.

- Click on a **complication location**.

- Wind the **Digital Crown** and move through the complications to pick one.

- Repeat the 2 steps prior to this for each individual complication location.

- Then exit the customization mode by pressing the **Digital Crown**.

- Click on the watch face when you are done.

How to Customize Watch Face Complications Using your iPhone

If it feels awkward to customize the complications on your Apple Watch, then you can make use of your iPhone.

- Open the watch app from your iPhone.

- Go to **My Watch and** then swipe right or left to choose a watch face.

- Click on a **complication location** you want to modify.

- Select one complication by scrolling through the available complications.

- Repeat the 2 steps prior to this for each individual complication location.

- The changes should reflect instantly on your Apple watch.

How to Customize Your iWatch to Wake to your Last Used App

The Apple watch is designed to show the time whenever you flick your wrist to wake your device. If you want the watch to take you straight to what you were doing before the watch went to sleep, follow the steps below to set this.

- Go to **Settings.**
- Click on **General.**
- Then select **Wake Screen.**
- Now navigate to **Screen Raise Show Last** section.

- On your screen, you would see the following options: Within 2 Minutes of Last Use, While in Sessions, Always and Within 1 Hour of Last Use.

- Choose your preference.

How to Make the On-Screen Text Larger

Follow the steps below to increase text size on your watch

- Go to settings.

- Click on **Brightness & Text Size.**

- Modify as suit your preference.

- If you are interested in having the time on the watch displayed in large numerals, select a Special Big text watch face.

How to Mute Alerts with your Palm

If sound is enabled on your device, you can prevent notification sounds from disturbing other people. When your alert comes up in places that does not entertain noise, use your hand to cover the display for about 3 seconds to mute any new sounds instantly. Follow the steps below to activate this feature.

- Go to the watch app on your iPhone device.

- Navigate to **My Watch.**

- Then click on **Sounds & Haptics**

- Finally, enable **Cover to Mute**.

How to Hide Watch Apps

To prevent 3rd party apps from displaying on your Apple watch,

- Go to the watch app on your iPhone device.

- Navigate to **My Watch.**

- Scroll to "**Installed on Apple Watch. "**

- Beside each apps you want to delete, move the toggle button to the left to Off
- The apps would still be installed on your iPhone except if you delete them from the iPhone.

How to Quickly Access VoiceOver and Zoom

If you want VoiceOver or Zoom to be quickly accessible on your watch, you can use the shortcut for triple-click Accessibility to automatically enable VoiceOver or Zoom.

- Go to the watch app stored on your iPhone device.

- Navigate to **My Watch.**

- Click on **General**

- Then select **Accessibility**

- And click on **Accessibility Shortcut.**

- Here, you can choose either **VoiceOver** or **Zoom** to activate when you triple click.

- You can also ask Siri to enable or disable VoiceOver with a simple voice command.

How to Take Screenshot

To take a screenshot on your Apple watch, quickly press down both the Digital Crown and the side button simultaneously

How to Force Restart Your iWatch

Continue to press and hold down the side button until the **Power Off** slider appears on your screen. Then pull the slider to the end of the screen.

How to Perform a Force Reboot

In case the screen of your watch is frozen, a hard reboot would help to reset the errors. Hold down both the Digital Crown and the side button for minimum of 10 seconds. Do not release until you see the Apple logo.

How to Save Custom Watch Faces

To save customized faces to be able to access them in the future,

- Force touch on the display of your device.

- Move to the left of your device, all the way down and then click on the new button.
- On the next screen, you can now customize the new watch face however you like.
- Swipe up to delete a custom watch face.

How to Set Your Watch to be 5 Minutes Fast

You can configure your watch to be 5 minutes ahead of the current time. This would have no effect on your notifications, alarms or even clocks from other countries.

- Go to settings.

- Click on **Time.**

- Then select **+0 min.**

- Use the **Digital Crown** to move the time forward, up to maximum of 59 minutes.

How to Turn Off Snooze for Your Alarms

If you would not want your alarm to give you an option to snooze, you can

deactivate the snooze option with
the steps below

- Go to the alarm app on your
  iWatch.

- Then click on the set alarm time
  you wish to modify.

- On the next screen, move the
  switch beside **Snooze** to the left
  to disable the option.

**How to Pre-compose Custom
Responses to Messages**

While you cannot type on your Apple
watch, however, you can create a few

pre-composed responses on your iPhone that you can click on in a conversation to auto send. Follow the listed steps below

- Go to the watch app on your iPhone device.

- Navigate to **My Watch.**

- Click on **Messages**

- Then select **Default Replies.**

- On the next screen, feel free to change the list, remove or add more pre-composed responses.

How to Always Send Dictated Text as Audio

When replying a message using your voice, your watch would give two options; either to send as an audio clip or as a dictated text. You can configure your watch to always send as audio clip or dictation without bringing up these two options again.

- Go to the watch app on your iPhone device.

- Navigate to **My Watch.**

- Click on **Messages**

- Click on **Audio Messages** and configure as desired.

How to Share your Location in Messages Using Force Touch

You can share your location with your friends at any time.

- Go to your message conversation.

- Fore touch/ press down on the display.

- Then click on **Send Location.**

How to Hold a Call Until you Find your iPhone

Although you can answer calls with your Apple watch, however it is usually not practical. If a call comes into your watch that you need to pick up but can't find your iPhone and you would rather not answer the call on your watch, click on **Answer on iPhone** to put the call on hold until you get your iPhone. The caller would hear a short-repeated message until you reach your phone.

How to Enable Walkie Talkie

If you need people to be able to reach you via the Walkie-Talkie feature on your iWatch, you would need to activate the feature.

- Launch the Walkie-Talk app on your iWatch.

- Then enable the **Available button** by moving the switch to the right.

How to Clear All Notifications Using Force Touch

I know that you can swipe left to delete single notifications from the screen, but its more productive to clear all notifications at once.

- Make a swipe down gesture from the display to show your notifications.

- Then press down/ force touch on the display to give the option for **Clear All.**

How to Flag Mail Messages with Force Touch

While you would not be able to create a new email on your Apple Watch, you can still flag messages to make it easy to reply later. To do this, press down on a mail message and then click on **Flag.**

How to Select the Mailbox that Shows on your iWatch

If you do not want to be notified from all your mailboxes, you can follow the steps below to choose a single mailbox you would like to receive notification on your Apple screen.

- Go to the watch app on your iPhone device.

- Navigate to **My Watch.**

- Click on **Mails.**

- Click on **Include Mail.**

- Choose your desired option on the next screen.

How to Switch Between Day and List Views in Calendar

If you want to see what day would be like while also viewing items you have in a list, simply switch between List View and Day View in the calendar app. You can achieve this with a force touch gesture inside the app.

How to Build Your Leaving time into Alerts from Calendar

If you have added a location to your event, you can set up an alert to notify you on the time to leave which would factor in walking or driving distance as well as traffic. First ensure that you have enabled the Travel time switch for each event with the steps below.

- Go to the calendar app on your iPhone.

- Click on the desired event.

- Then go to **Edit.**

- And enable the **Travel Time** option.

How to Use Taptic Engine to Get Directions

The iWatch uses buzzes, beeps and movements to alert you but this is not just for notifications alone. The Taptic engine can also be used to find your way around a city. When using the Apple watch to get directions, the iWatch would tap you whenever you need to take a turn.

- To take a left turn, you would get 2 taps played 3 times, that is, tap-tap for 3 times.

- To make a right turn, the watch would notify you with 12 steady taps.

- When you get to the last leg of your journey, you would feel a long vibration as well as when you get to your destination.

How to Use Force Touch to Stop Directions

You can always force touch at any part of the Map app to stop receiving directions.

How to Set a Default Location for Your Weather Details

The weather app on the iWatch can present details from several cities including your present location. Follow the steps below to set a default location

- Go to the Apple watch app on your iPhone.

- Click on **My Watch.**

- Navigate to **Weather.**

- Then click on **Default City** in the next screen and set as desired.

How to Preview iPhone Photos from your Apple Watch

The iWatch allows you to use its camera app as a remote display and shutter for photos as well as to quickly preview any shots you took recently. This way, you can always confirm you have the perfect shot before picking your iPhone.

Close Your Exercise Rings

Your iWatch throughout the day would encourage you to close your exercise rings. Whenever you want to see how you are doing, simply launch the Exercise app.

Check Your ECG

You can now check your ECG with your iWatch.

- Click on the ECG app on your iWatch.

- For approximately 30 seconds, hold your finger on the digital crown for electrical signals to be measured.

Use the iWatch to Concentrate

The in-built Breath app helps you to relax. Set the duration of breaths you wish to track in minutes, then click on **Next** and relax.

How to Pair Your iPhone with another iWatch

You can pair another watch to your iPhone similar to how you paired the first one with the steps below

- Go to the Apple watch app on your iPhone.

- Click on **My Watch.**

- Click on your current iWatch at the screen top.

- Then click on **Pair New Watch.**

How to Switch Between iWatches Automatically

After you have paired an additional Watch to your iPhone, you can then easily switch between the two watches.

- Go to the Apple watch app on your iPhone.

- Click on **My Watch.**

- Click on your Apple Watch at the screen top.

- Beside the option for **Auto Switch,** move the slider to the right to enable the feature.

- So, whenever you want to switch, just take off one and wear the other.

- Then lift your wrist to wake the device,

Note: all paired Apple watches share their activity data so you need not worry about loss of data when switching.

How to Switch Between iWatches Manually

The steps below would show you how to manually switch the paired watches

- Go to the Apple watch app on your iPhone.

- Click on **My Watch.**

- Click on your Apple Watch at the screen top.

- Then click on the second watch you wish to switch to,

- You would then see an orange circle that has a white checkmark beside the chosen iWatch.

Chapter 7: Conclusion

Now that you have known all there is to know about your Apple Watch series 5, I am confident that you would enjoy operating your new smart device.

All relevant areas concerning the usage of Apple watch and watchOS 6 has been carefully outlined and discussed in details to make users more familiar with its operations as well as other information not contained elsewhere.

If you are pleased with the content of this book, don't forget to recommend this book to a friend.

Thank you.

Other Books by the Same Author

- iPhone 11 User Guide

  https://amzn.to/2mBZOME

- iPhone 11 Pro Max User Guide

  https://amzn.to/2lSEBOc

- iOS 13 User Guide

  https://amzn.to/2nxY9Yw

- Beginner's Guide to iPadOS

  https://amzn.to/2O2w7VJ

- Mastering your iPad 7th gen

  https://amzn.to/2oAIVmh

- Apple TV 4K/ HD User Guide

  https://amzn.to/2kqpBq4

- Amazon Echo Dot 3rd Generation User Guide

  https://amzn.to/2kE3X1T

- Kindle Oasis 3 10th Generation User Guide

  https://amzn.to/2kGM42w

- Mastering your iPhone XR for beginners, seniors and new iPhone users

  https://amzn.to/2mgegtc

- Samsung Note 10 and Note 10 Plus User Guide

  https://amzn.to/2mjBTRG

- Fire TV Stick User Guide

  https://amzn.to/2kQwTDP